THIS COLORING BOOK BELONG TO:

_____

_____

_____

_____

Lion

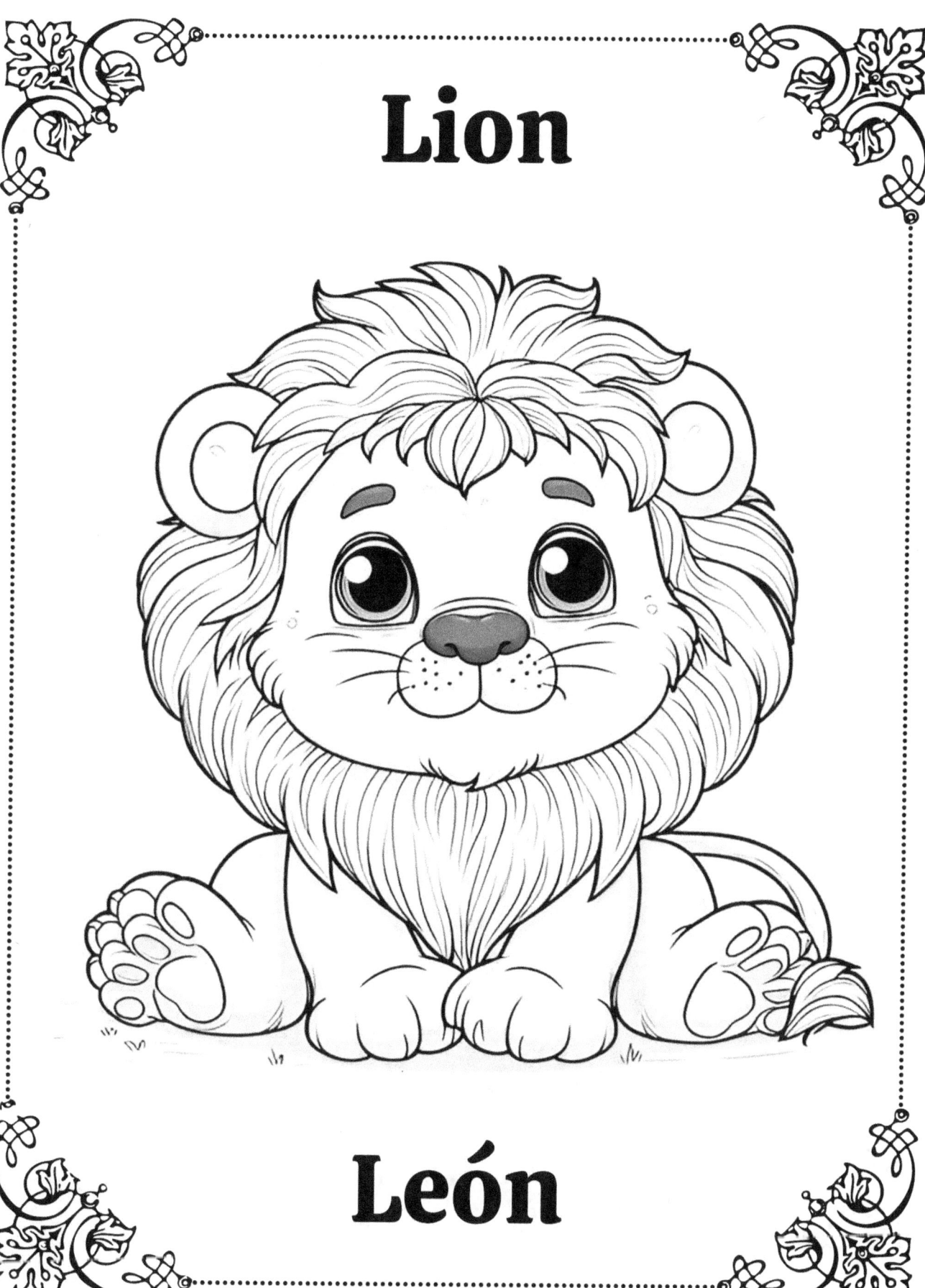

León

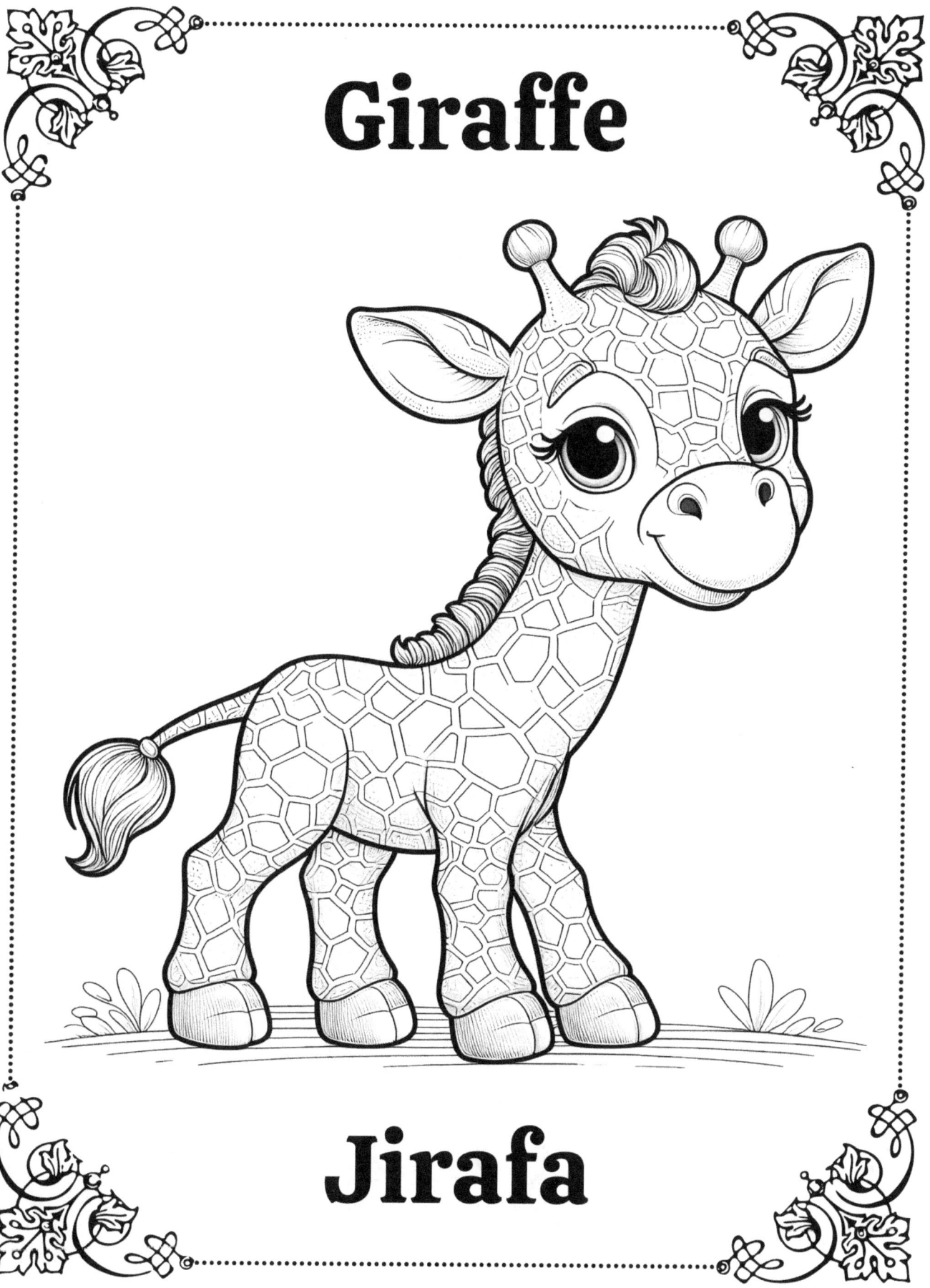

Zebra

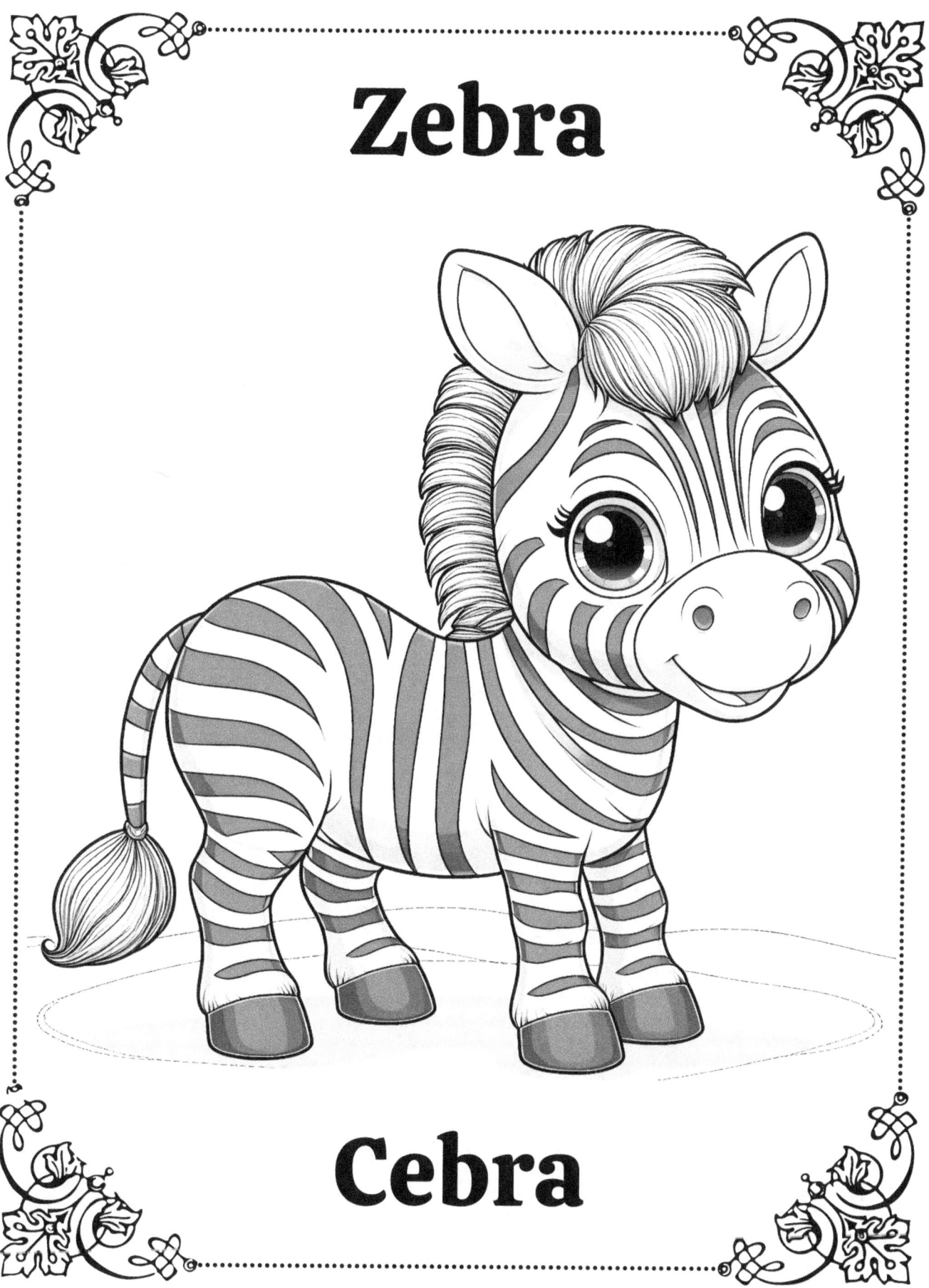

Cebra

Cheetah

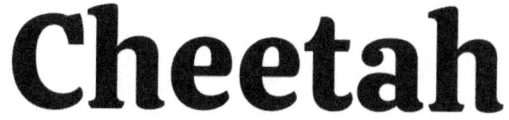

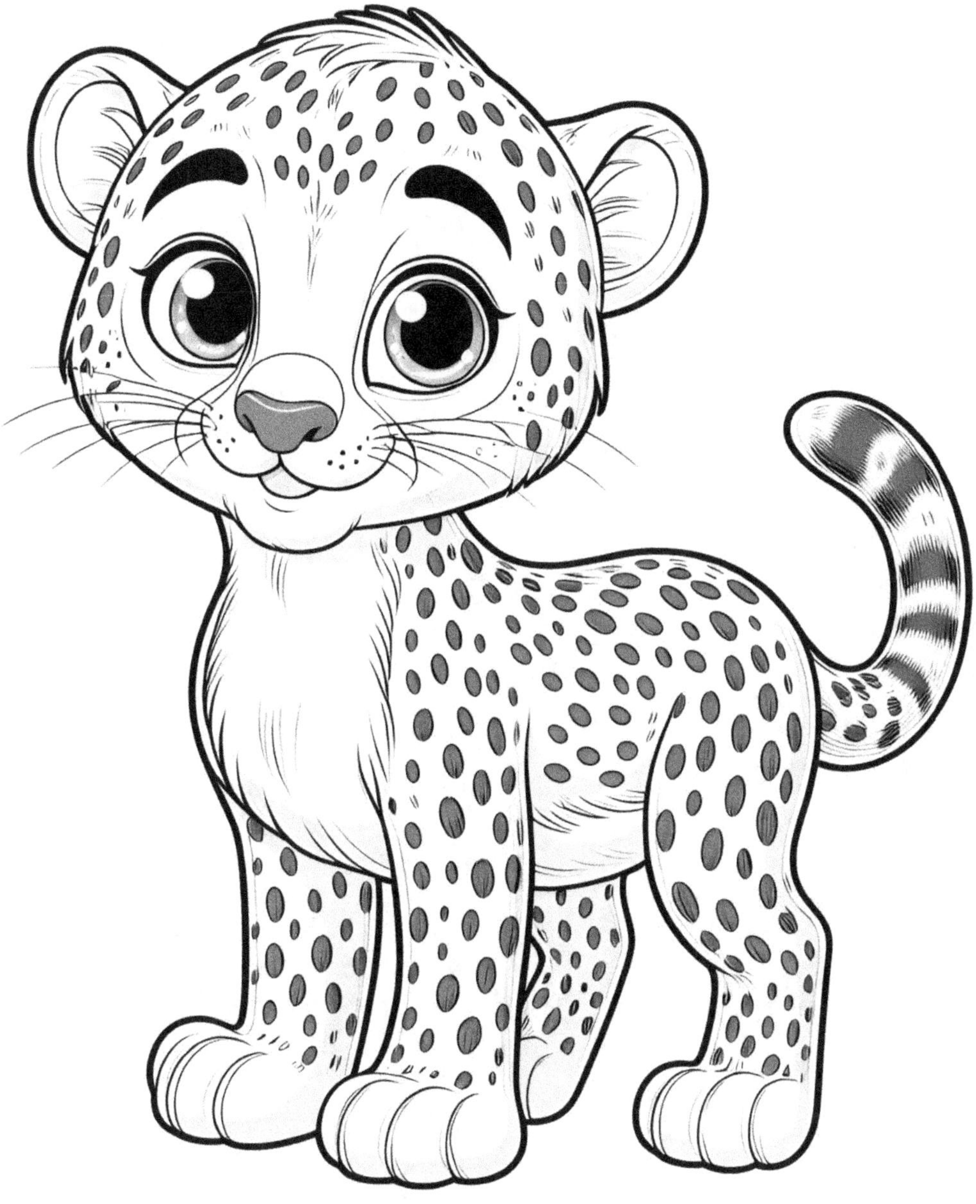

Guepardo

Elephant

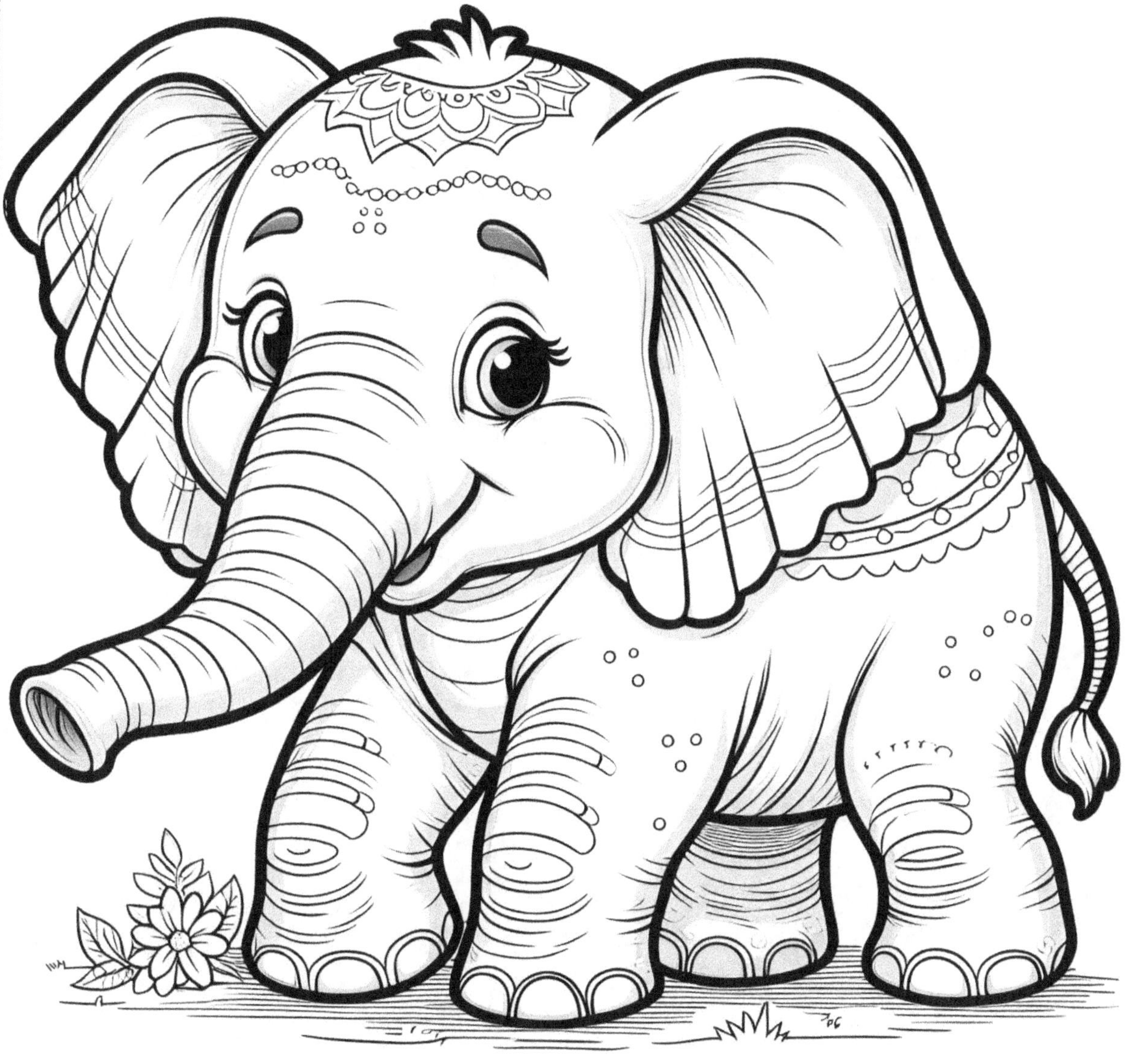

Elefante

Tiger

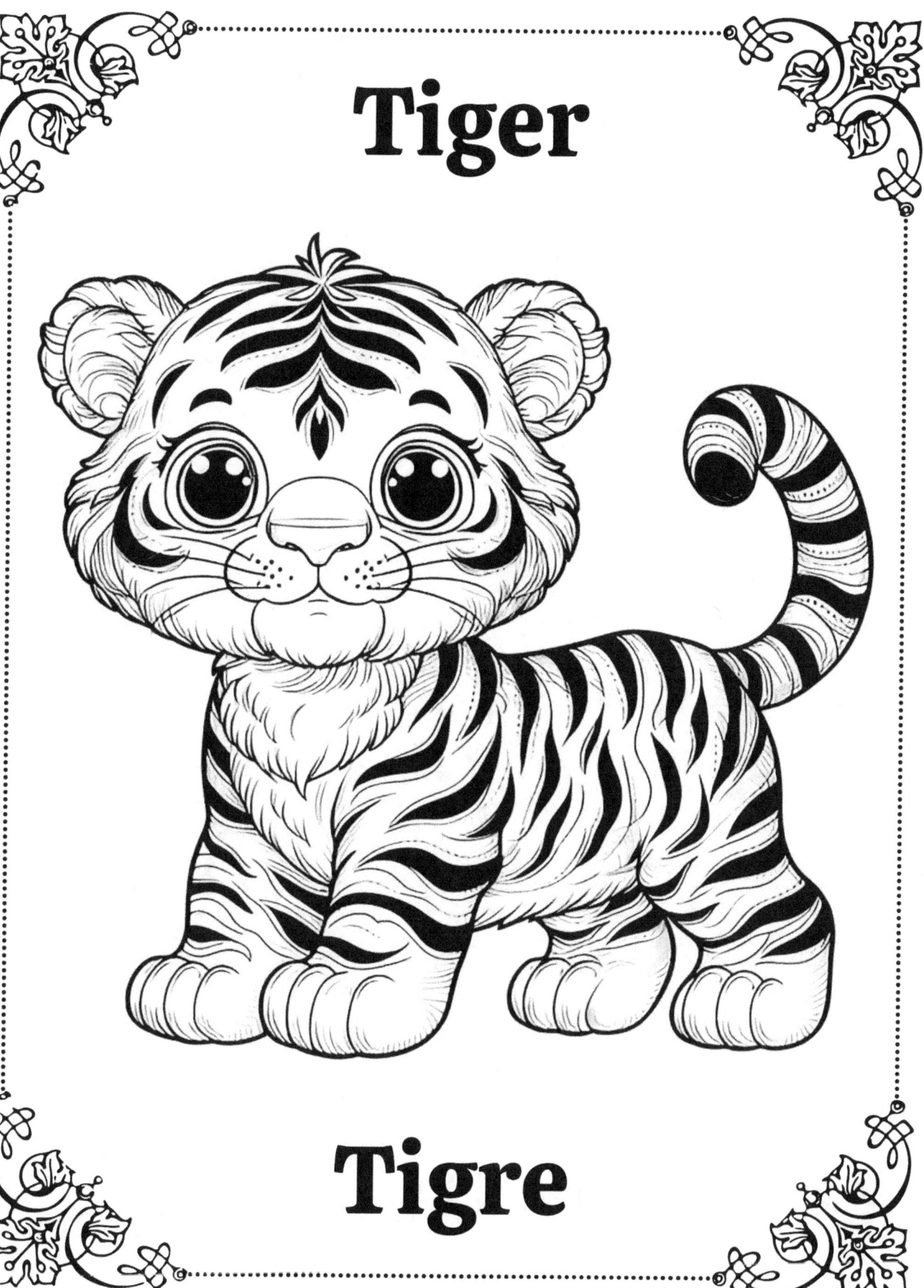

Tigre

Panda

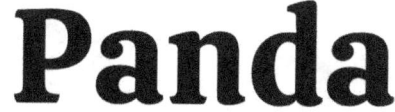

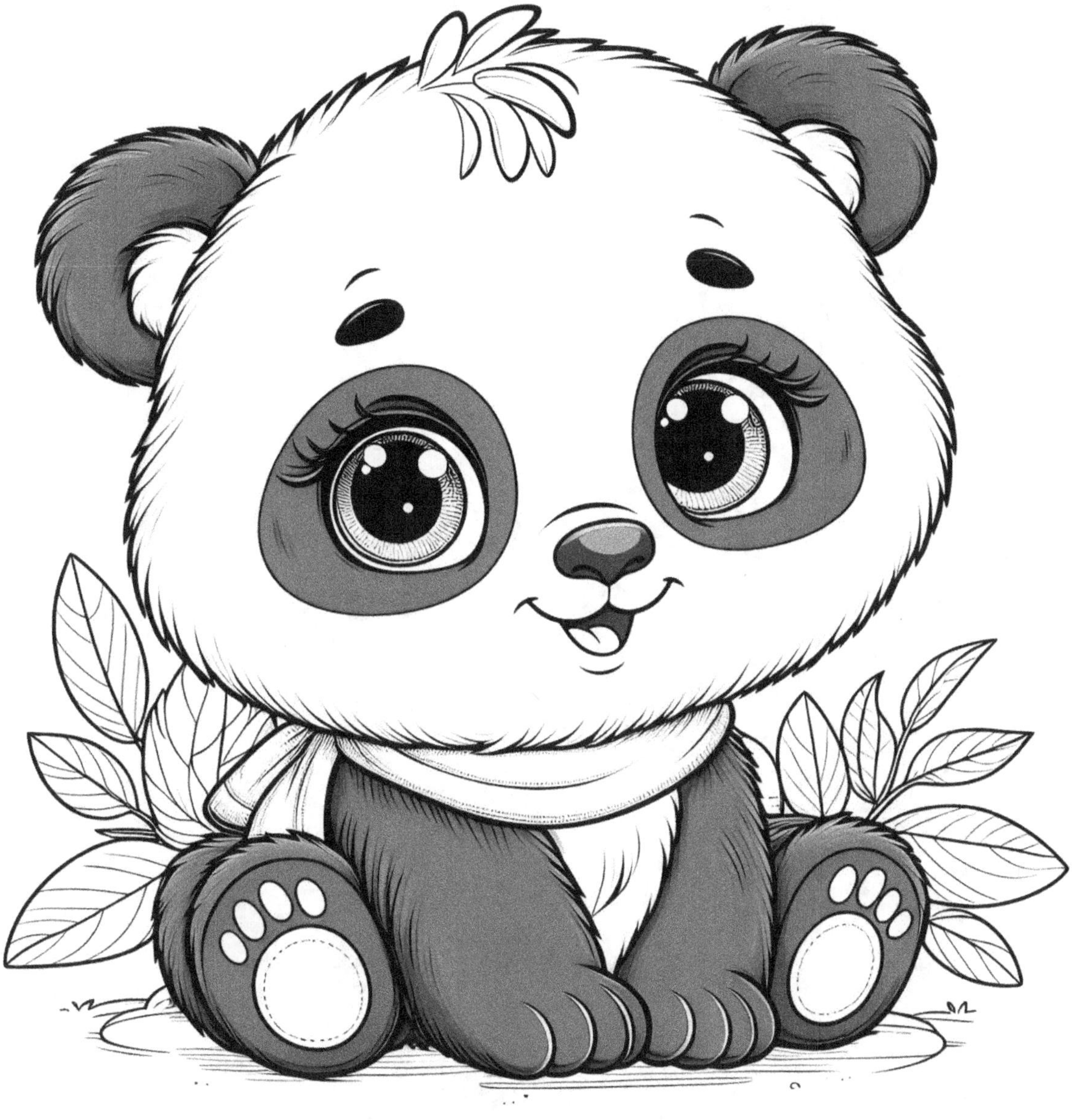

Panda

Bear

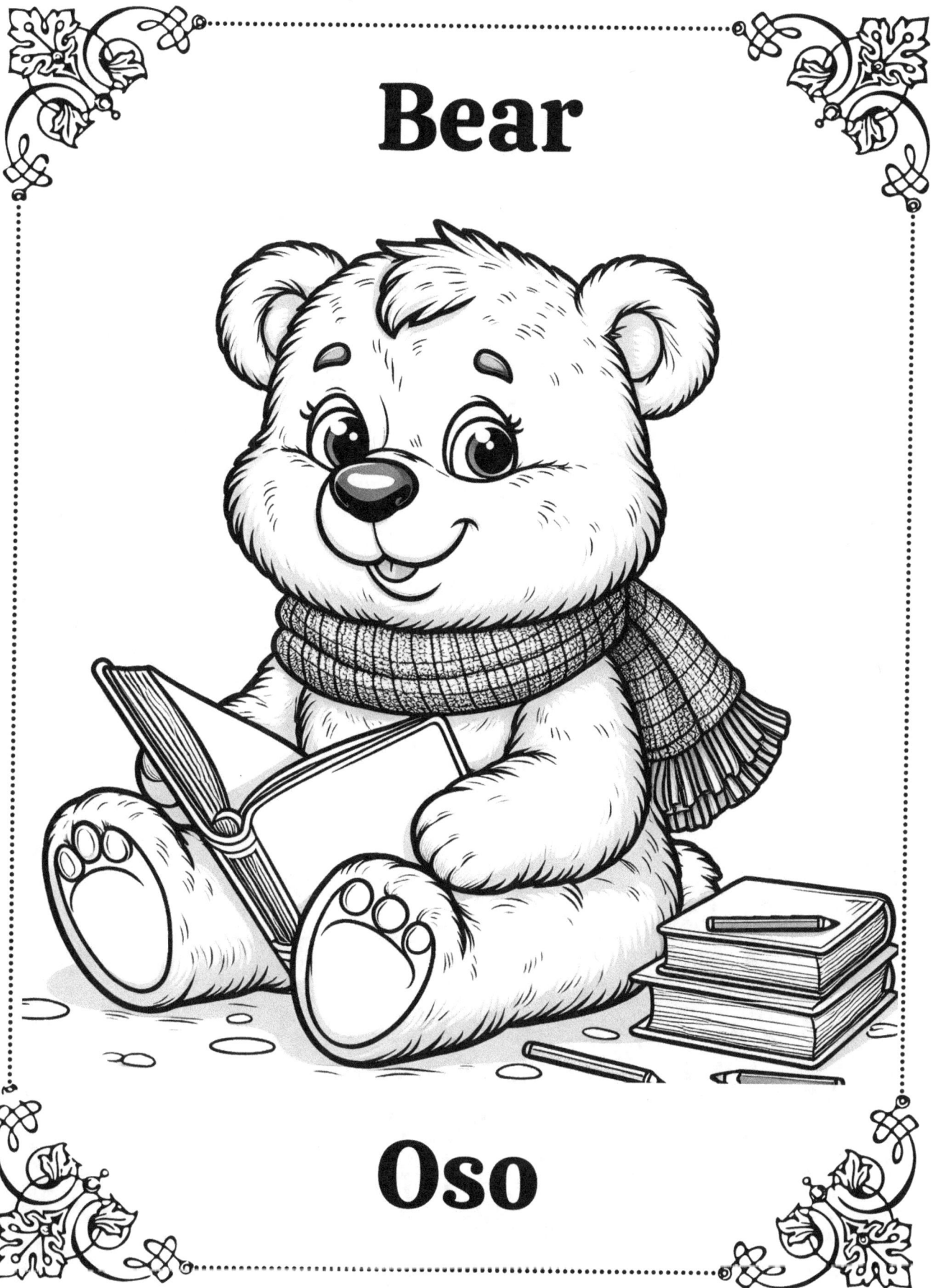

Oso

Deer

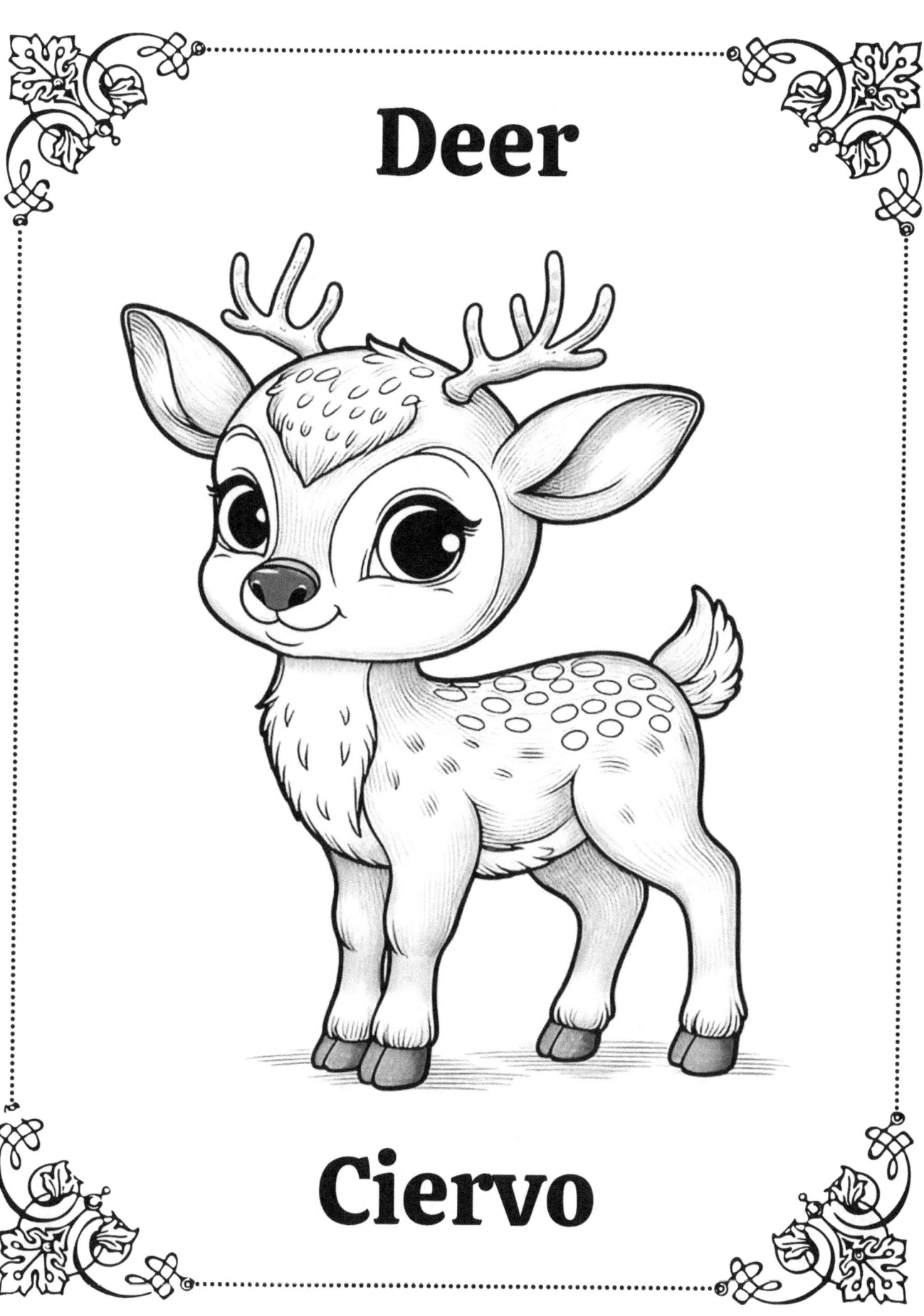

Ciervo

Fox

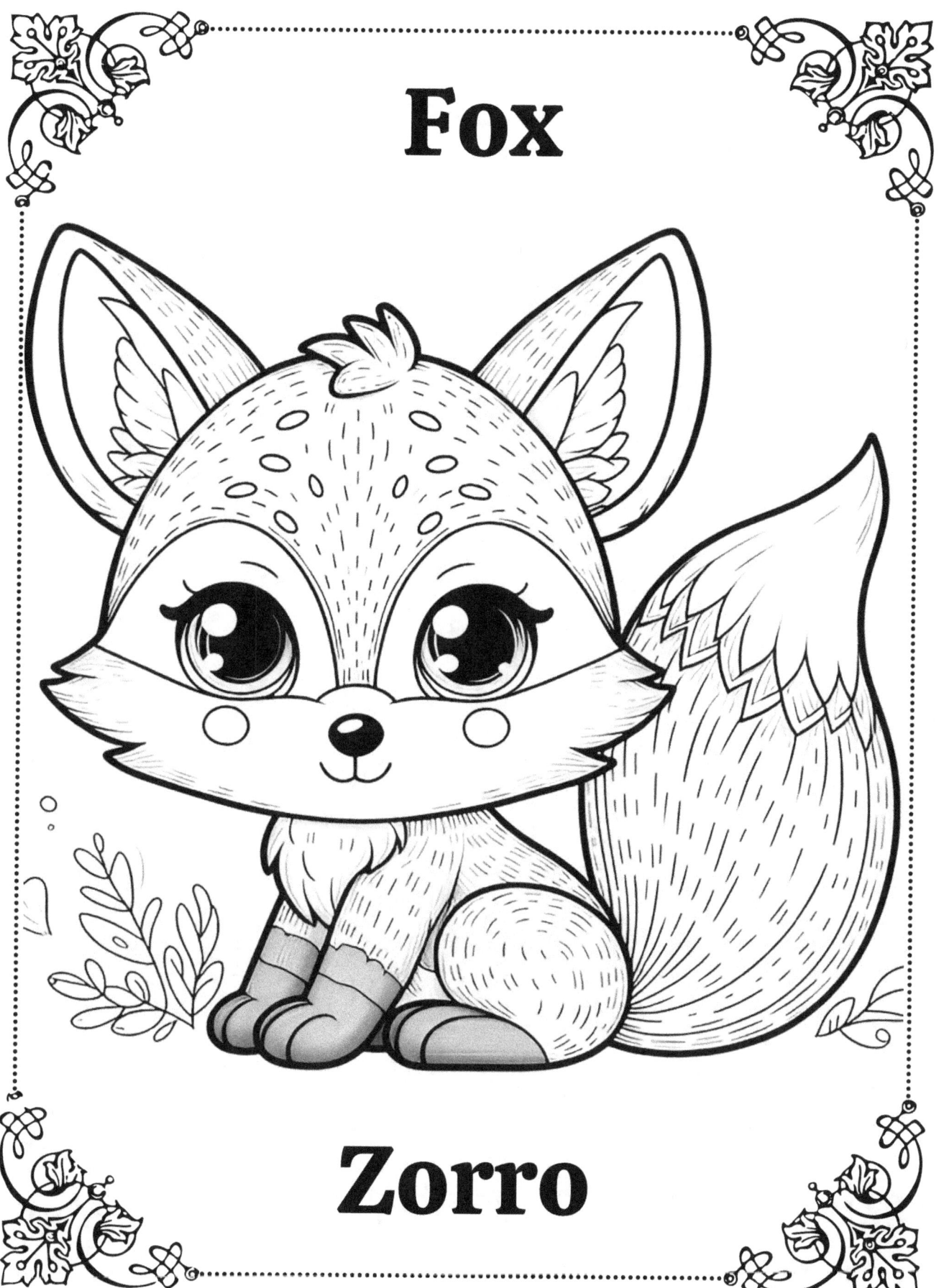

Zorro

Rhino

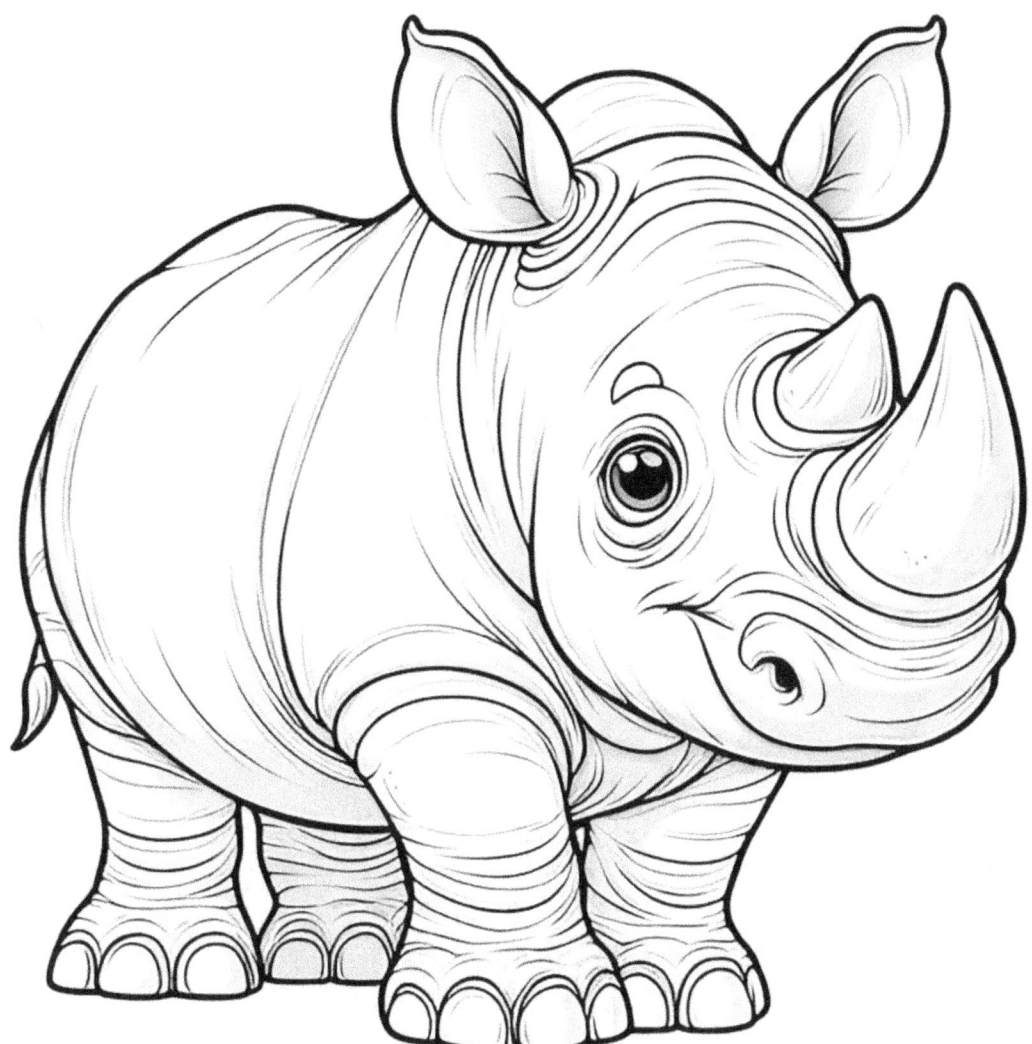

Rinoceronte

Wolf

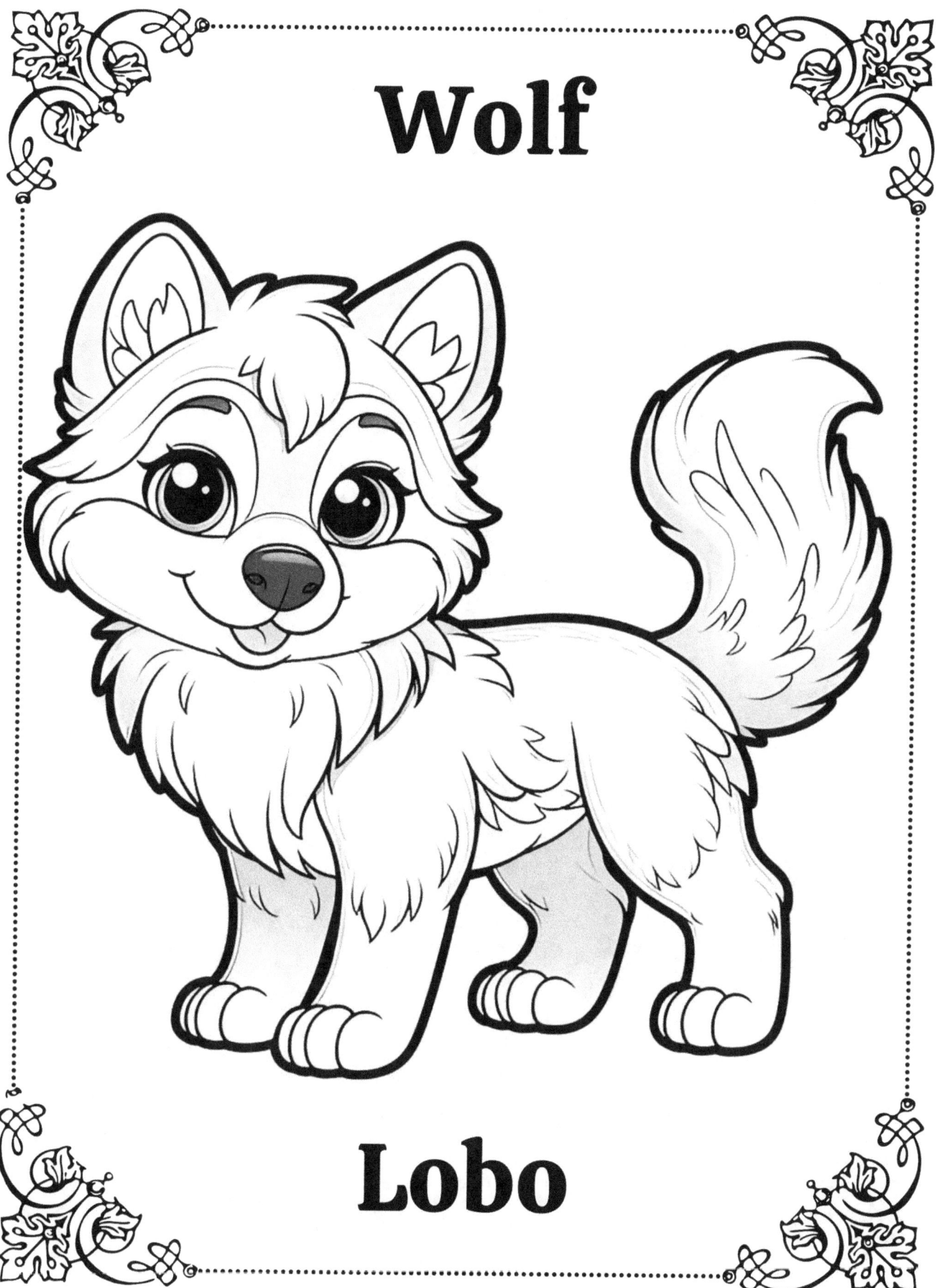

Lobo

Gorilla

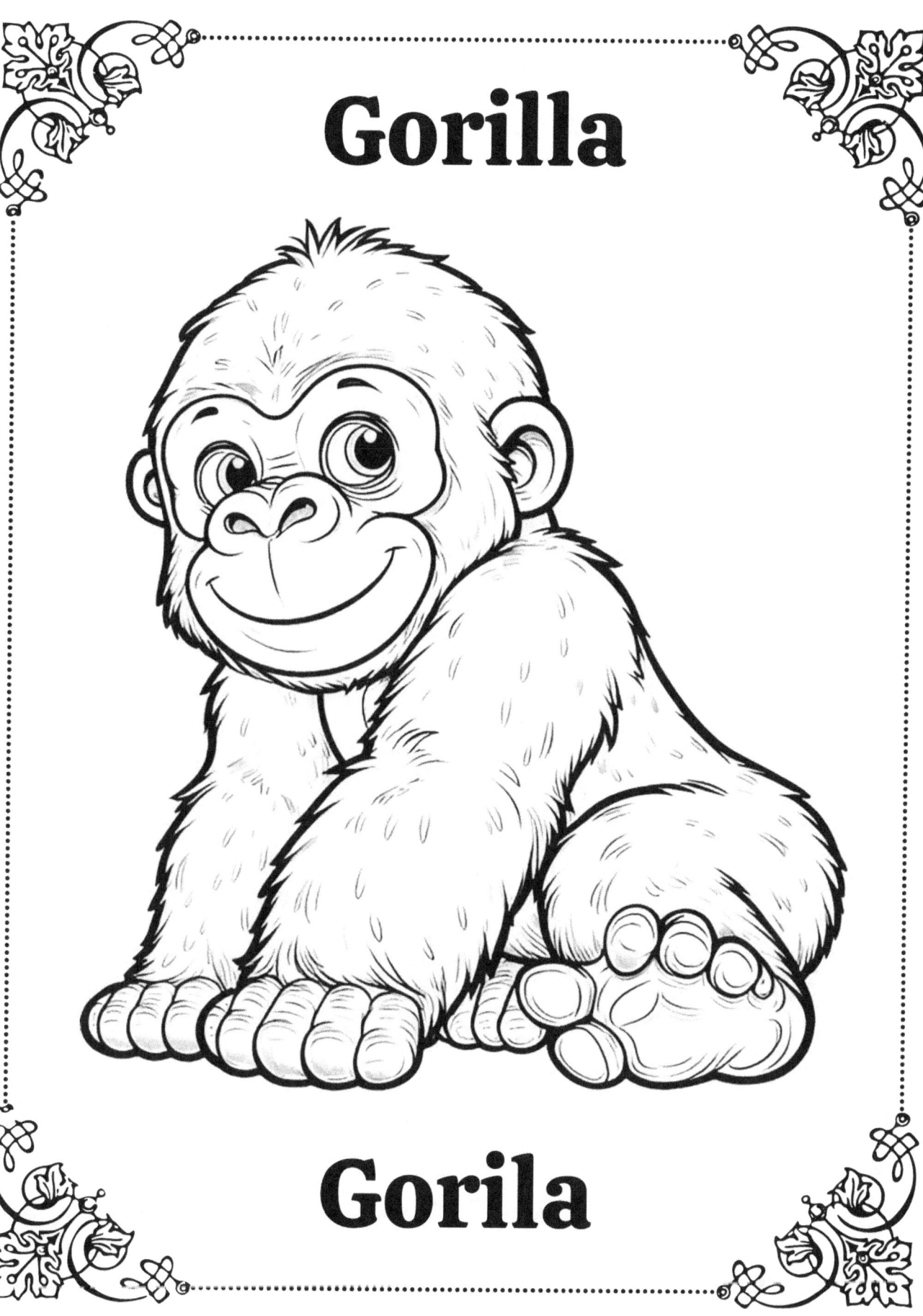

Gorila

Koala

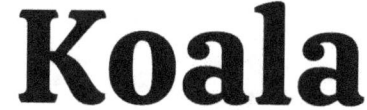

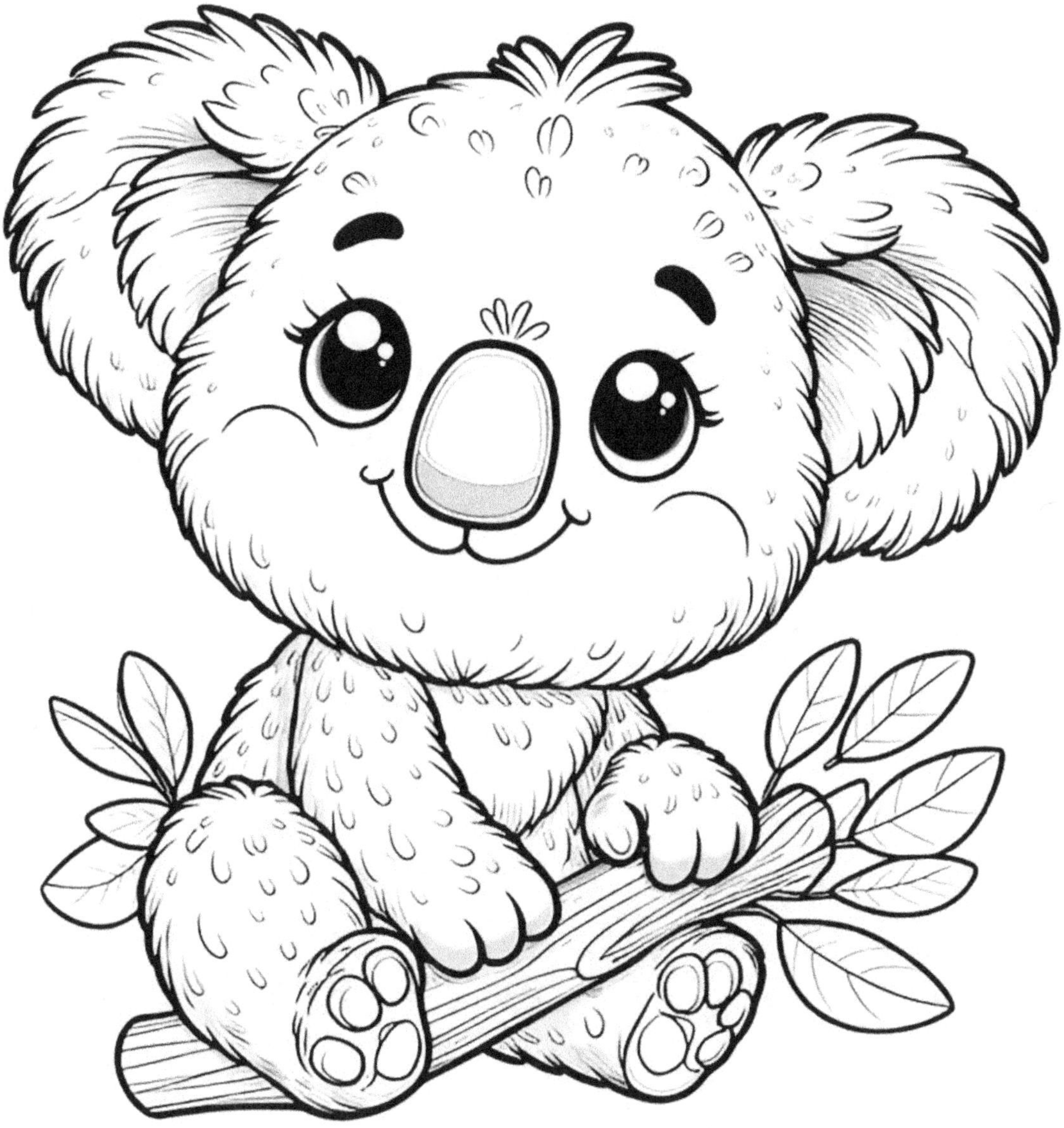

Koala

Hyena

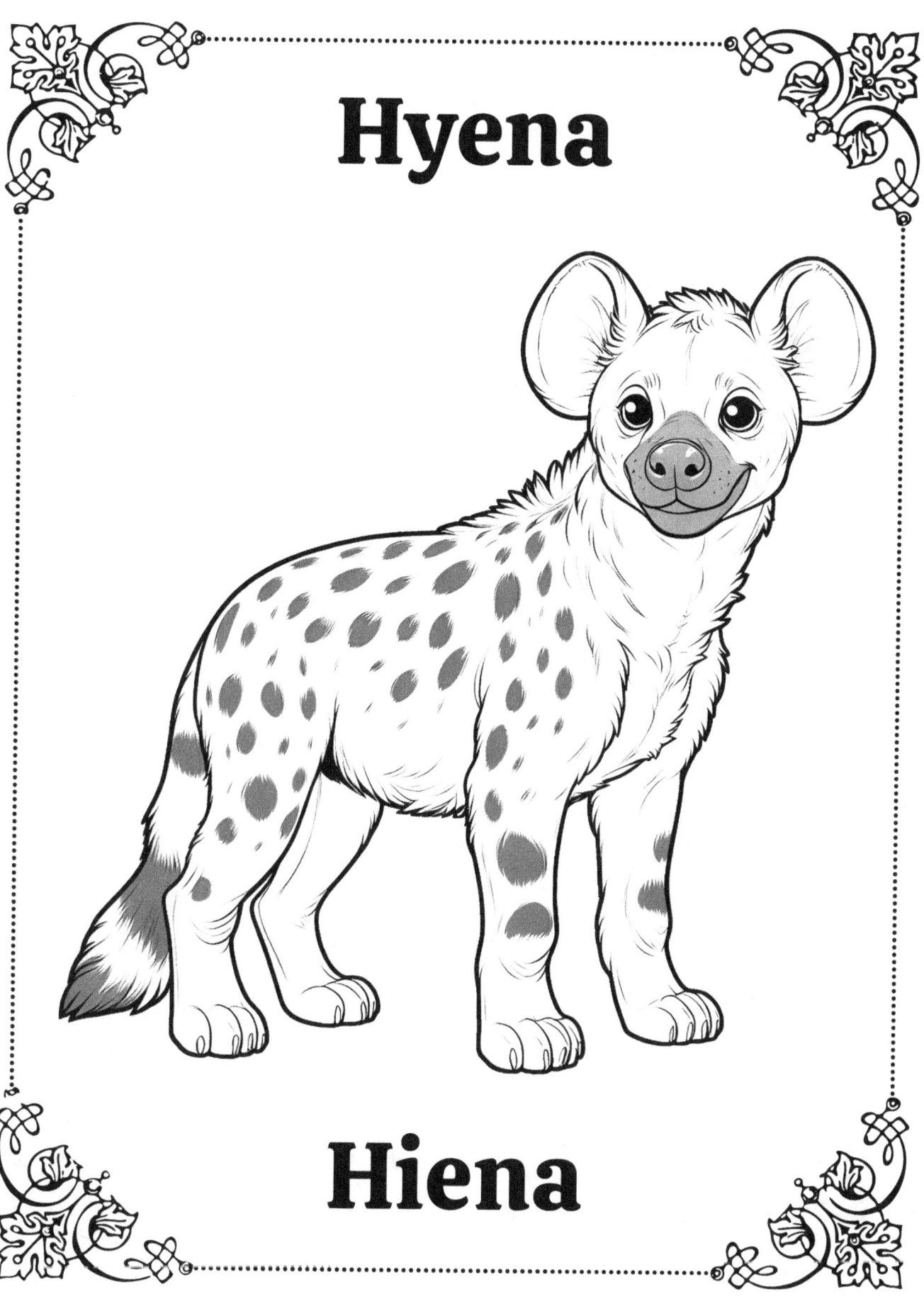

Hiena

www.ingramcontent.com/pod-product-compliance
Lightning Source LLC
Chambersburg PA
CBHW081021240526
45471CB00018B/3936